I'm Two, I'm Two!

I'm Two, I'm Two!

by Valerie Carlson Pressley
Illustrated by Kayla Lynn Olson

ABOOKS
Alive Book Publishing

Additional copies may be ordered from the publisher
for educational, business, promotional or premium use.
For information, contact ALIVE Book Publishing at:
alivebookpublishing.com, or call (925) 837-7303.

ISBN 13
978-1-63132-099-6

Library of Congress Control Number: 2020912381

Library of Congress Cataloging-in-Publication Data
is available upon request.

First Edition

Published in the United States of America
by ALIVE Book Publishing
an imprint of Advanced Publishing LLC
3200 A Danville Blvd., Suite 204, Alamo, California 94507
alivebookpublishing.com

PRINTED IN THE UNITED STATES OF AMERICA

10 9 8 7 6 5 4 3 2 1

For Georgia and Logan

I'm Two, I'm Two! How old are *you*?
C'mon let's go,
there is so much to do!

I'm running and jumping
and hopping away.
Sometimes too fast,
but I just love to play.

Dolls and cars, trains and kites.
Just a few of the toys
that I really like.

I love to play dress-up and wear
Mommy's shoes.
The red ones or blue ones?
She lets me choose.

I can recognize numbers
and count them out loud.
I just counted to 10!
Oh, I am SO proud.

I also sing songs
and say nursery rhymes.
Especially my ABCs, I do those
a million, zillion times.

A B C D E

F  G H I J

K L M N O

P Q R S  T

U V W X Y

Z

I have a few friends
and we play hide-n-seek.
I've found a secret spot,
so please don't peek!

I love to laugh, stomp in puddles,
spin and twirl.
If it sounds like fun, heck,
I'll give it a whirl.

I'm showing my talents
at the potty training thing.
Can you imagine the freedom
that undies will bring?

There seems no end
to all I can do and see.
I love being Two,
but just can't wait to be Three!

Also by Valerie Carlson Pressley

I'm Here, I'm Here!
I'm One, I'm One!

ABOOKS

ALIVE Book Publishing and ALIVE Publishing Group
are imprints of Advanced Publishing LLC,
3200 A Danville Blvd., Suite 204, Alamo, California 94507

Telephone: 925.837.7303
alivebookpublishing.com

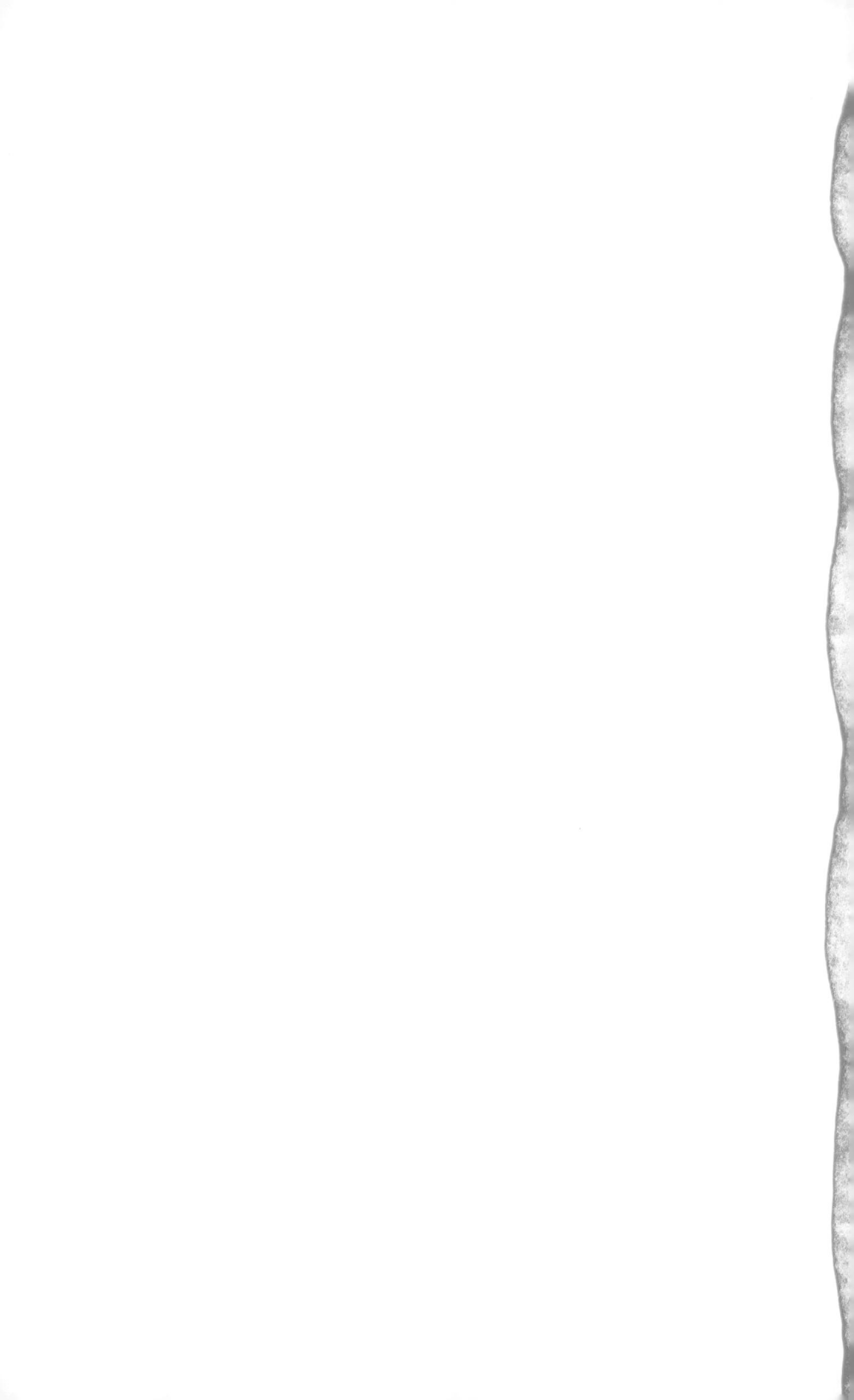

9 7 8 1 6 3 1 3 2 0 9 9 6